JUMP THROWS AND CURTAIN CALLS

BASEBALL'S MOST SIGNATURE
MOVES, CELEBRATIONS, AND MORE

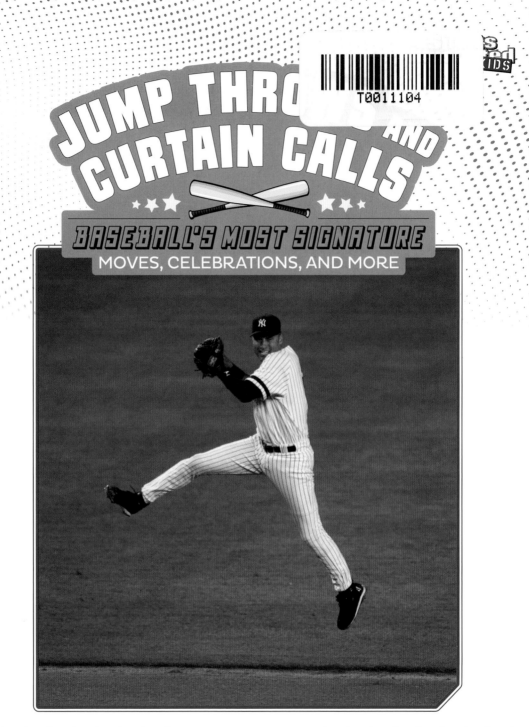

by Steve Foxe

CAPSTONE PRESS
a capstone imprint

Published by Capstone Press, an imprint of Capstone
1710 Roe Crest Drive, North Mankato, Minnesota 56003
capstonepub.com

Library of Congress Cataloging-in-Publication Data
Names: Foxe, Steve, author. Title: Rally caps and curtain calls : baseball's most signature moves, celebrations, and more / by Steve Foxe.
Description: North Mankato, MN : Capstone Press, [2024] | Series: Sports illustrated kids. Signature celebrations, moves, and style | Includes bibliographical references and index. | Audience: Ages 9-11 | Audience: Grades 4-6 | Summary: "Young baseball fans discover the sports' most signature moves and celebrations in this dynamic book from Sports Illustrated Kids. Derek Jeter's jump-throw. Ichiro Suzuki's mobile swing. Reggie Jackson's iconic curtain call. These are some of baseball's most signature moves and celebrations! In this high-interest book, discover the history behind these moves and many more-from the athletes who made them famous to their history within the game. Created in collaboration with Sports Illustrated Kids, Rally Caps and Curtain Calls will be a surefire homerun for young readers and sports fans"-- Provided by publisher.
Identifiers: LCCN 2023027855 (print) | LCCN 2023027856 (ebook) | ISBN 9781669065623 (hardcover) | ISBN 9781669065579 (paperback) | ISBN 9781669065586 (pdf) | ISBN 9781669065609 (kindle edition) | ISBN 9781669065593 (epub)
Subjects: LCSH: Baseball--Miscellanea--Juvenile literature. Classification: LCC GV867.5 .F69 2024 (print) | LCC GV867.5 (ebook) | DDC 796.357--dc23/eng/20230818
LC record available at https://lccn.loc.gov/2023027855
LC ebook record available at https://lccn.loc.gov/2023027856

Editorial Credits
Editor: Donald Lemke; Designer: Kayla Rossow; Media Researcher: Svetlana Zhurkin; Production Specialist: Katy LaVigne

Image Credits
Associated Press: 8, 28, Mark J. Terrill, 23; Getty Images: Al Bello, cover, 1, Allsport/Tom Hauck, 15, Dilip Vishwanat, 11, Ezra Shaw, 5, 20, Jeff Gross, 19, Jonathan Daniel, 12, Len Redkoles, 25, MLB Photos, 24 (bottom), MPI, 6 (bottom), Otto Greule Jr., 16, 17, Transcendental Graphics, 9; Newsroom: Heritage Images/Historica Graphica Collection, 7; Shutterstock: DarkPlatypus (dotted wave), back cover and throughout, DELstudio (baseball), 8 and throughout, Michal Sanca (baseball player), 4 (top) and throughout, vectorisland (baseball bat), cover, 1; Sports Illustrated: Walter Iooss Jr., 27; Superstock: ClassicStock, 4 (bottom)

All internet sites appearing in back matter were available and accurate when this book was sent to press.

★★★★★★★★★★★★★★★★★★★★★★★★★

TABLE OF CONTENTS

Words in **bold** are in the glossary.

SIGNATURE BASEBALL

Baseball is one of the world's most popular sports. People started playing it in England long ago. Then it became famous in the United States. It is now known as America's **pastime**.

Derek Jeter

Throughout the history of the sport, some baseball players have stood out. These players are often known for their unique moves, styles, or ways of celebrating.

CALLING THE SHOTS

Babe Ruth is a baseball legend. He won four World Series during his 15 years with the New York Yankees. Perhaps his most famous moment at bat happened during the 1932 World Series.

Babe Ruth played for the New York Yankees from 1920 to 1934.

By the fifth inning of Game 3, the score was tied 4–4 between the Yankees and the Chicago Cubs. Then Ruth stepped up to the plate.

Babe Ruth nears home plate after hitting a home run during the 1932 World Series.

With two strikes, Ruth held up his bat.

Many thought he was pointing to center field.

When Ruth swung a third time, he hit a home

run. The Yankees won!

SWING, BATTER, SWING!

During his career, Hall of Fame player Ken Griffey Jr. was known for his home-run records. He was also famous for the way he swung his bat. Since then, many players have copied his swing, but few can master it.

Ken Griffey Jr. played for the Seattle Mariners, Cincinnati Reds, and Chicago White Sox.

The key to Griffey's swing was balance and smoothness. He stood upright at the plate. His follow-through was one motion.

The most famous part of his swing was the one-handed finish. After Griffey hit the ball, he dropped his left hand. His right hand followed through with the bat.

CAREER STATS

Ken Griffey Jr.
Batting Average: .284
Home Runs: 630
Runs Batted In: 1,836

BACK TO FRONT

Ichiro Suzuki played baseball for nine years in his home country of Japan before heading to the Seattle Mariners in 2001. Ichiro was one of the first Japanese players to have a successful career in America too. But some coaches overlooked Ichiro because of the way he batted.

Ichiro played his final Major League game on March 21, 2019, at the Tokyo Dome in Japan.

Ichiro at a practice in 2001

Most hitters keep their weight on their back foot. But Ichiro's swing has been described as a "**pendulum**." He started with his weight on his back foot. But he shifted to his front foot mid-swing.

Ichiro won Rookie of the Year after his first year. He went on to receive many other awards and honors. Still, very few players shift their weight during a swing the way Ichiro did.

CATCH SOME AIR

Some of baseball's most **iconic** moves are defensive plays. Derek Jeter is one of the top-ranked shortstops in Major League Baseball (MLB) history. He perfected his **signature** jump throw while in the Minor Leagues.

Derek Jeter won 5 Gold Glove awards during his MLB career.

Derek Jeter performs his signature jump throw in 2002.

When a ball hit the field near Jeter, he scooped it up in a **backhanded** motion. Then he jumped, spun his shoulders toward first base, and threw the ball to the first baseman.

The move sped up the time it took to catch the ball and throw it to his teammate. Every second counts on the field. This move is now called the "Jeter Jump Throw"—no matter who does it.

TORNADO TIME

Many players like to put their own spin on baseball moves. Pitcher Hideo Nomo was known for one of the most unique windups in the game. During his career, Nomo raised both hands in the air. Then he turned his body until his back faced the batter. Finally, he whipped around to release the ball.

Nomo's windup earned him the nickname "Tornado."

FIELD-WORTHY FACIAL HAIR

Some players become famous for their signature style. During the 1970s, seven-time All-Star Rollie Fingers helped bring respect to **relievers**. He also stood out for his unusual handlebar mustache!

More recently, pitcher Brian Wilson grew a long, jet-black beard. Many fans grew beards of their own. They would chant "Fear the Beard!" during Wilson's games.

ONE-OF-A-KIND MOMENTS

On October 18, 1977, Reggie Jackson of the New York Yankees hit three home runs in a row in a single World Series game. He is the first and only MLB player to ever accomplish this feat!

Jackson earned the nickname "Mr. October" for his legendary World Series performances.

Jackson waves to fans during the 1977 World Series.

After each home run, Jackson walked out of the dugout. He waved his cap at the crowd. He thanked the fans. This "curtain call" became Jackson's signature celebration.

Each season, MLB players break records. Some will win World Series rings. But only a few players will ever be remembered for their signature moves, celebrations, and style.

GLOSSARY

backhanded (BAK-han-duhd)—using the back of the hand or a backward motion

iconic (eye-KAHN-ik)—famous and easy to recognize

pastime (PASS-tym)—fun thing we do when we're not working or at school

pendulum (PEN-juh-luhm)—something that swings back and forth from a fixed point

reliever (rih-LEE-vuhr)—a baseball player who helps the starting pitcher when they are tired or not playing well

signature (SIG-nuh-chur)—special and easy to recognize

READ MORE

Berglund, Bruce. *Baseball GOATs: The Greatest Athletes of All Time.* North Mankato, MN: Capstone, 2022.

Buckley Jr., James. *It's a Numbers Game! Baseball: The Math Behind the Perfect Pitch, the Game-Winning Grand Slam, and So Much More!* Washington, D: National Geographic Kids, 2021.

Driscoll, Martin. *Homers and Hot Dogs: Behind the Scenes of Game Day Baseball.* North Mankato, MN: Capstone, 2023.

INTERNET SITES

Major League Baseball
mlb.com

National Baseball Hall of Fame: Baseball History, American History and You
baseballhall.org/baseball-history-american-history-and-you

Sports Illustrated Kids: Baseball
sikids.com/baseball

INDEX

ABOUT THE AUTHOR

Steve Foxe is the Eisner and Ringo Award-nominated author of over 75 comics and children's books including *X-Men '92: House of XCII*, *Rainbow Bridge*, *Adventure Kingdom*, and the Spider-Ham series from Scholastic. He has written for properties like Pokémon, Mario, LEGO City, Batman, Justice League, Baby Shark, and many more. He lives somewhere cold with his partner and dog and is a Detroit Tigers fan for life.